D1226390

TO THE EXTREME

Snowboarding

by Matt Doeden

Reading Consultant:
Barbara J. Fox
Reading Specialist
North Carolina State University

Capstone
press

Mankato, Minnesota

Blazers is published by Capstone Press
151 Good Counsel Drive, P.O. Box 669, Mankato, Minnesota 56002
www.capstonepress.com

Library of Congress Cataloging-in-Publication Data
Doeden, Matt.
    Snowboarding / by Matt Doeden.
    p. cm.—(Blazers. To the extreme)
    Includes bibliographical references and index.
    ISBN 0-7368-2731-5 (hardcover)
    1. Snowboarding—Juvenile literature. [1. Snowboarding.
2. Extreme sports.] I. Title. II. Series: Doeden, Matt. Blazers. To the
extreme.
GV857.S57D64 2005
796.93'9—dc22   2003026628

Summary: Describes the sport of snowboarding, including tricks and
    safety information.

Editorial Credits
Angela Kaelberer, editor; Jason Knudson, designer; Jo Miller,
    photo researcher; Eric Kudalis, product planning editor

Photo Credits
Corbis/AFP, 20; David Stoecklein, 14; Duomo, 7, 12, 21;
    Duomo/Chris Trotman, 16–17; Jeff Curtes, 28–29; Reuters
    NewMedia Inc., 15
Getty Images/Agence Zoom, 25; Al Bello, 11; Brian Bahr, 9;
    Clive Brunskill, 5; Donald Miralle, 8; Ezra Shaw, 6; Gary M. Prior,
    cover; Jed Jacobsohn, 19
Mark Gallup, 22, 23, 27
SportsChrome Inc., 13

1 2 3 4 5 6 09 08 07 06 05 04

Table of Contents

Snow and Speed

A snowboarder glides down
a long ramp made of snow. She
builds speed and glides up one
side of the ramp.

The rider leaps into the air at the top of the ramp. She does a full spin in the air.

The rider lands the trick. The crowd cheers. She has just won an Olympic gold medal.

Snowboards

Most snowboards are made of fiberglass and wood. The boards are strong, flexible, and lightweight.

Bindings are attached to the top of the board. The bindings keep the feet in place.

Bindings

Freestyle rider

Freestyle riders choose short, wide boards because these boards are stable. Racers ride long, narrow boards because they are fast.

Racer

Slalom Snowboarder Diagram

Bindings

Board

Slalom pole

Helmet

Goggles

Tricks

Ramps made of snow or wood
help freestyle riders do tricks in the
air. These tricks are called aerials.

Many riders do grabs. Riders use
one or both hands to grab a part of
the board.

BLAZER FACT

In 1997, the X Games
sports competition used
200 tons (181 metric tons)
of manufactured snow.

Riders do spins and flips in the air. They combine spins and flips with grabs to create new tricks.

safety

Snowboarders wear helmets and
goggles. Helmets protect their heads
during falls. Goggles shield their
eyes from the sun and snow.

Many ski resorts have places just for snowboarders. Snowboard parks are another safe place to ride. Riders can stay safe while they have fun.

Sliding the rail

Rail

Glossary

aerial (AIR-ee-uhl)—a trick performed in the air

binding (BINE-ding)—a strap that holds the feet of a rider on a snowboard

fiberglass (FYE-bur-glass)—a strong, lightweight material made from thin threads of glass

freestyle (FREE-stile)—a snowboarding style that includes tricks and jumps

goggles (GOG-uhlz)—glasses that fit tightly around the eyes

slalom (SLAH-luhm)—a downhill race in which riders weave through sets of poles

Read More

Brown, Gillian C. P. *Snowboarding.* X-treme Outdoors. New York: Children's Press, 2003.

Firestone, Mary. *Extreme Halfpipe Snowboarding Moves.* Behind the Moves. Mankato, Minn.: Capstone Press, 2004.

Herran, Joe, and Ron Thomas. *Snowboarding.* Action Sports. Philadelphia: Chelsea House, 2003.

Internet Sites

FactHound offers a safe, fun way to find Internet sites related to this book. All of the sites on FactHound have been researched by our staff.

Here's how:

1. Visit *www.facthound.com*
2. Type in this special code **0736827315** for age-appropriate sites. Or enter a search word related to this book for a more general search.
3. Click on the **Fetch It** button.

FactHound will fetch the best sites for you!

Index